The Bridal Banquet

The Bridal Banquet

Holy Communion for House Churches and Small Groups

Robert Schmidt

WIPF & STOCK · Eugene, Oregon

THE BRIDAL BANQUET
Holy Communion for House Churches and Small Groups

Copyright © 2025 Robert Schmidt. All rights reserved. Except for brief quotations in critical publications or reviews, no part of this book may be reproduced in any manner without prior written permission from the publisher. Write: Permissions, Wipf and Stock Publishers, 199 W. 8th Ave., Suite 3, Eugene, OR 97401.

Wipf & Stock
An Imprint of Wipf and Stock Publishers
199 W. 8th Ave., Suite 3
Eugene, OR 97401

www.wipfandstock.com

PAPERBACK ISBN: 979-8-3852-6045-4
HARDCOVER ISBN: 979-8-3852-6046-1
EBOOK ISBN: 979-8-3852-6047-8

VERSION NUMBER 10/08/25

Scripture quotations are from New Revised Standard Version Bible, copyright © 1989 National Council of the Churches of Christ in the United States of America. Used by permission. All rights reserved worldwide.

To the beloved memory of Karin,
courageous companion in international service

Contents

Preface | ix

Acknowledgments | xiii

Introduction | xv

Chapter 1   We Are the Bride of Christ | 1
Chapter 2   The Guest List | 8
Chapter 3   The Menu | 15
Chapter 4   The Host and Servers | 22
Chapter 5   The Banquet Hall | 29
Chapter 6   Banquet Gifts | 37
Chapter 7   Sharing the Meal | 45
Chapter 8   The Wedding | 56

Conclusion | 61

Appendix | 63
Bibliography | 67

Preface

THE FIRST TIME I celebrated Holy Communion in Nigeria as a newly ordained pastor in Nigeria I began to wonder about the practice. There had not been time to learn the local language, so I had to memorize the words of institution in a foreign tongue. That day I communed hundreds of people who had waited months for the celebration. I knew none of them and their teachers and elders had decided who would be admitted to the Lord's Supper. As a twenty-four-year-old from a nation thousands of miles away they had to wait for me to do this.

Attending the service were the elders from several congregations. Before becoming Christians, they had been involved in clan ceremonies that had lasted for days. It was not easy for them to become Christian, but they had matured in the faith and were fully capable of administering communion. During the Nigerian Civil War, when the missionaries left and the teachers who had read sermons had gone back to their villages, these elders encouraged the members of their churches during the devastation the war brought to their villages. During those terrible years their churches grew as people found comfort and help in their faith. Those elders, male and female, were fully capable of celebrating

PREFACE

and administering the Lord's Supper. If that was true then, it might be true now and everywhere.

At our missionary training we read Roland Allen's book *Missionary Methods: St. Paul's or Ours*. In it he described how St. Paul trusted the elders of the new churches to celebrate communion as a regular part of their worship. Addressing missionary churches in distant lands, Allen's ideas were largely dismissed. Missionaries wanted native clergy trained so that they might be replaced by native-born speakers and leaders. While evangelists might witness and preach in gatherings and congregations, only an ordained pastor could administer communion. As a result, most pastors and authorities in the younger churches around the world maintain the custom of limiting the administration of communion to theologically trained, ordained pastors.

However, in some nations where the Christian church is persecuted, or at least limited, people are worshiping in homes. Often there are no pastors around. People gather around the word of God for their devotion and prayers. House churches have also been increasing in Europe and America, bringing together people who have left their churches and those who never wanted to join. Some may have communion, others may not. Without theologically trained leaders questions have arisen about some of the beliefs and practices of such house churches. Are there biblical teachings and emphases that might be useful in these communion celebrations? Given the experience at my first communion in Africa, and the potential of a more biblical practice of celebrating the Lord's Supper, perhaps this little volume on the Lord's Supper may be of some help.

I was not moved to write this little book to argue for the superiority of house churches over denominational congregations. I believe that God has done wonderful things through those larger institutions and will continue to do so. Rather, I hope to bring the blessings of the word of God and Holy Communion to the many who have left the congregations but are still hungry for the spiritual nourishment they had in the past. To those who are attracted to house churches, this booklet is for them.

PREFACE

Internationally, it is also for those house churches in nations where the church is limited or even persecuted. In many poor nations house churches may be the final form of Christian communities or merely the first step in the development of larger congregations. In either case the Lord's Supper can be a vital part of their spiritual growth and ongoing church life.

To keep the celebration of the Lord's table simple and easy to pass on, I have limited the number of footnotes in the text. However, in the appendix, I have listed much of the material supporting the positions taken in the text.

Acknowledgments

THIS BOOK WAS MADE possible through the biblical insights of Roland Allen and conversations with his grandson, Hubert Allen. International perspectives have come from the Roman Catholic missionary Vincent Donovan, working with the Masai in Africa, and Dayanand Bharati, a Christ Bhakta in India.

Special thanks are also due to the Lutheran Lay Assistants in Alaska and the Northwest who served isolated communities and congregations that could not afford a pastor. Thanks are also due to the leaders of the regional church, Erhart Bauer, Warren Schumacher, and Paul Linnemann, who blessed their efforts.

A faculty house church at Colorado State University also gave me a personal perspective on the beauty and significance of that worship and outreach. This book owes much to Sidney and Erik Thompson who worked hard to bring it about and made it such a worshipful experience.

Introduction

THE MEAL WAS ALMOST over and a young man with us asked, "Why is this meal different from others?" The lady of the house explained, "We are going to finish this meal by celebrating the Lord's Supper. We are going to remember what Christ has done for us on the cross, and as we eat this bread and drink this wine we are going to receive Christ in our bodies, minds, and hearts." She continues, "Think of this as a 'bridal banquet' preparing us to be joined with Christ in heaven and now, nourishing us with his body and blood for forgiveness, community, and the strength to lead a better life."

Most of the people around the table had left the churches in which they had been raised and where they had worshiped. Several Catholics had been deeply offended when they heard about the sexual abuse of Native American children in boarding schools, compounding the disgrace of priests molesting children in their parishes. Some evangelicals left their churches when it seemed that right-wing politics had replaced the gospel. An older couple from a dying church had left because it took all of their strength to keep up the building and there was no time left to help people. Several were there simply because they were friends and curious.

Some had participated in small groups' Bible studies. Those, however, had not included communion. In nearly every church, celebrating the Lord's Supper was the responsibility and privilege of the pastor, priest, or preacher, nearly all of whom were professional clergy. This meant that unless one was connected to an organized congregation and its pastor, one might not partake of the meal that Christ urged, "This do, in remembrance of me."

This has always been a problem for isolated rural communities without a church. Now, in the modern world, who will commune the truck drivers, the medical workers in war-torn areas, and the exhausted aid workers in refugee camps around the world? Previously church officials, defending church practices, have said that though the Lord's Supper was beneficial, it was not necessary. However, as more small churches are forced to close because they cannot afford a pastor, as more Christians leave the church without leaving their faith, it is time to take another look at going back to the New Testament practice of celebrating the Lord's Supper in small groups, in homes, in refugee camps, and wherever Christians need the strength to continue.

This is not a new idea. Thousands of house churches already exist throughout the world. Many are in lands that are hostile to organized churches. Others have been started to reach out to the unchurched in largely secular cultures. Still others have grown out of neighborhood Bible studies. Some of these house churches have communion services; others do not. Christians from more liturgical churches with a high view of communion, calling it a sacrament and referring to it as the Eucharist, may not be comfortable with communion in a casual setting. Yet, there is a precedent for small group communion even in those churches as it is celebrated at the bedside for members of these churches. Military chaplains share communion with a platoon in war.

Coming out of a liturgical church Martin Luther wrote extensively about the liturgy in the Latin *Formulae Missa* and the *Deutsche Messe*. However, in addition to these two services he wrote:

> The third kind of service which a truly Evangelical Church Order should have would not be held in a public place for all sorts of people, but for those who mean to

INTRODUCTION

be real Christians and profess the Gospel with hand and mouth. They would record their names on a list and meet by themselves in some house in order to pray, read, baptize, receive the sacrament and do other Christian work.[1]

Luther, however, said that he did not have the desire to work on such a house church, nor did he have anyone who really desired that type of service. However, with the growth of house churches today, it is evident that there are many who desire that type of a worshiping community. Now is it possible for people from both liturgical and nonliturgical churches to meet together around the Lord's table in a reverent and meaningful way? In a more missional setting than Luther knew, might the Lord's Supper be a means of grace, bringing forgiveness and the assurance of salvation to outsiders?

Questions and Answers

Can any group of Christians, regardless of their theology, traditions, and background, simply have the Lord's Supper together? Can anyone, like the lady of the house, just administer and celebrate Holy Communion? Should it be held at a regular meal? If so, how would that meal be different from any other? Who should be invited to come? Would it just be for Christians, or should it also be for the curious? If it is at a refugee camp, might it be for the refugees as well as the truck drivers and the staff? Would there be any common features of such communions, or would one celebration be unrecognizable from any other? Are there patterns for such communions that can be copied and adapted to the situation in which we find ourselves?

The purpose of this book is to attempt to answer these questions so that with a clear conscience those who have left the church or who have lived without it can receive Christ and his promises in the Lord's Supper. Some church bodies might have strong objections to such practices based upon their theology of the Eucharist or the Lord's Supper, yet we will attempt to show, on the basis of

---

1. Luther, *Luther's Works* 53:63–64.

INTRODUCTION

the Scripture, ecumenical dialogue, history, and the growing house church movement, that such communions are valid and necessary.

The Bridal Banquet

For those raised in the tradition of a high Eucharist, coming respectfully to the altar and kneeling to receive Christ's body and blood, a house church communion, hosted by a mother or brother, might seem to trivialize the sacrament. Even those who have communed in their pews when the bread and wine are passed might retain the feeling that the Lord's Supper is really a church thing not to be mixed up with salad and baked beans at the dining room table. To accent the importance and eternal significance of the sacrament done in homes and informal gatherings we have called it the *bridal banquet*.

To underscore the Lord's Supper as a banquet rather than a snack, this little volume highlights the groom and bride and what their marriage covenant has to do with our identity, community, security, and future. Mining Paul's admonitions in Corinth, the parables of Christ, and the church in Acts, we have also come up with a guest list for the banquet. Then of course there is the menu, not an easy task given the different tastes of those from different traditions. What will be the banquet halls for the traveling saints building homes for the indigent, feeding the hungry, and just coming home tired from work? Who will be the hosts? Are they qualified? Would they know what they are doing?

Some banquets have programs, small sheets of paper that tell us what is going to happen and in what order. A chapter of this book contains suggested programs (liturgies?) for the Lord's Supper. Each one is addressed to situations in which we might find ourselves, from an ordinary work week to preparation for an emergency in which we might lose our lives. Reflecting on Paul's admonition to the Corinthians, what would a communion be like between masters and servants, the well-to-do, and the homeless? Would it also include people of different confessions and traditions?

INTRODUCTION

In this treatment of house church communions, we are in no way arguing that they replace traditional communion services in churches. Nor is this an effort to maintain that house churches are superior to regular organized congregations. In fact, the lessons for these house church communions might also trigger meditative thoughts while communing in regular churches as well. How are we tied to those with whom we disagree? What does this sacrament mean as we struggle with an emergency? What does it mean when we just need to let go and not think of anything but let Christ take over? Yes, just like always, our sins are guaranteed forgiveness by Christ himself.

A bridal banquet is only important because it anticipates the marriage to come. The book concludes by contemplating Christ's death and resurrection as a model for our own. The view of being joined with Christ for eternity imparts real significance to our bridal banquets. Although they may seem ordinary, they contain within them the divine appetizers of the marriage feast to come. This keeps us hopeful even in the midst of personal, church, and world crises.

Chapter 1

We Are the Bride of Christ

THIS CHAPTER'S TITLE IS quite a statement considering who the groom is. Paul writes to the Colossians, "He is the image of the invisible God, the firstborn of all creation; for in him all things in heaven and on earth were created, things visible and invisible, whether thrones or dominions or rulers or powers—all things have been created through him and for him" (Col 1:15-16). A bridal banquet with him is no trivial thing; it is an honor and then some. This banquet is better than a banquet with the president. Communing with the very image of God lends significance, dignity, and importance to the meal. Yet as Christ's own bride, we are loved and welcomed and assured of his faithfulness in the promise of our marriage. We belong at the banquet.

A bridal banquet, however, is also sobering. For one thing, partaking of the meal, there is a pang of doubt. Does the bridegroom know of our previous lovers, when we were seduced by false gods posing as belief systems, a love of worldly stuff, and sin? But we still belong at the banquet. Paul writes, "God was pleased to reconcile to himself all things, whether on earth or in heaven, by making peace through the blood of his cross. And you who were once estranged and hostile in mind, doing evil deeds, he has now reconciled in his fleshly body through death, so as to present you holy and blameless and irreproachable before him" (Col 1: 20–22).

The bridal banquet is also sobering for another reason. Is this the guy for us? Do we want to spend the rest of our lives with him? Though he is attractive he also has high standards. Will be able to work things out when bad stuff happens? Will this marriage work? Will we put up with him and he with us? What is it like being married? We have seen bad relationships before. Are we going to be part of one of those? When questions like that cross our minds we need to know more about how the groom sees the marriage covenant.

The Marriage Covenant

God is a covenant maker. These constitutional agreements were made with Noah, Abraham, and the Hebrew slaves coming from Egypt. God begins covenants as he helps people. He saved Noah and his family from the flood and blessed and multiplied their children. To Abram and Sarah, he gave a son and promised descendants would be more than the stars in the heavens. For the slaves in Egypt, he liberated them and provided for their desert journey.

How are people reminded of the vows they made on their wedding day? Maybe it is a visit to the place where they first fell in love. Maybe it is their anniversary. God also wanted his people to remember the covenants. Rainbows continue to glow in the sky. For each covenant he gave a sign to ratify the covenant. God placed a rainbow in the sky for his covenant with Noah (Gen 9:13). Circumcision was the sign of God's covenant with Abraham (Gen 17:11). When God made his covenant with the Hebrew slaves there was also a sign which ratified the covenant between God and his people. After the people agreed to their part of the covenant Moses built an altar at the base of Mt. Sinai. Animals were sacrificed and half of the blood was dashed on the altar and the other half on the people. Then Moses said, "See the 'blood of the covenant' that the Lord has made with you" (Exod 24: 4–8).

At the first Lord's Supper Jesus passed the wine and said, "This is the new covenant in my blood" (Mark 14:24). Here is an anniversary of the marriage covenant between Christ and us. Jesus' words make this clear when he says, "Do this in remembrance of me" (Luke 22:19). Love in any relationship is often proved when you see what your partner has given up showing love to you. As we remember the blood Jesus shed on the cross for us, we thankfully rest and rely upon the covenant of his love.

The "new blood of the covenant" also recalls the blood sprinkled on the mercy seat of the ark of the covenant which was for the forgiveness of sins of the whole people of God on the Day of Atonement. Jesus said, "This is my blood of the covenant, which is poured out for many for the forgiveness of sins" (Matt 26:28). One of the problems of any marriage or friendship is that we can fail to live up to our part of the relationship. We are forgetful, careless, or even cruel. Only repentance and forgiveness can bring things back together. Thankfully we receive Christ's forgiveness and love in his Supper.

Spoken at the Passover, the disciples could not miss the significance of Christ's mention of his blood. At the Passover the blood of a lamb was smeared on the doorposts of the house and the angel of death passed over that house. The blood of the Lamb saved people from death. At the same time, because of the carnage in Egyptian homes, the liberation of the slave people had begun, and they were free. As people receive the blood of the covenant in the wine at the Lord's Supper they too are liberated. Now they are no longer enslaved to guilt that comes from breaking laws, even God's laws. Now they are free.

They were also to take with them unleavened bread that would not mold on the long journey ahead. At the Passover Jesus used such unleavened bread when he said, "This is my body, which is given for you. Do this in remembrance of me" (Luke 22:19). In the Passover setting it meant that this unleavened bread will keep you alive. As the body of Christ, this unleavened bread can signify that Christ will keep you alive in all the challenges ahead in life, and in death. And when the unleavened bread was eaten,

God provided more bread in the manna the children of Israel found in the desert. That, too, kept them alive in the almost impossible trials of the wilderness.

Bridal Banquet in a Broken World

What a contrast! This banquet is so different from the broken worlds we live in. Fears fuel politics across the globe. Wars are never far away. They are fought over wealth, power, unemployment, racial and religious hatred, and random violence. Heat, drought, and floods are increasing every year. Massive debt leads to failing states; hunger and thirst afflict their children. Refugees struggle to escape poverty and conflict only to be denied entrance to safety and hope.

Within this broken world churches, synagogues, mosques, and temples remain question marks. They are often used to promote even more divisions. At times Christians gloss over those love passages so that they can elevate themselves as arbiters of right and wrong. Should Christians impose their beliefs on people raised in different traditions? Must Jews always back the state of Israel regardless of its policies? Will Muslims defend the use of terror as a legitimate definition of *jihad*? Is it right for Hindu nationalism to persecute Muslims, Sikhs, and Christians? While millions are nurtured by the excellent teachings of their faiths, religions have become fertile ground for their leaders and politicians to sow divisions and hatred.

Most of us can ignore these problems of our world until its troubles invade our personal lives. Families struggle over limited resources. Children no longer want to go to church. Lots of young people are depressed. Will artificial intelligence mean the end of our jobs? Will refugees and immigrants threaten our way of life? With what seems to be increasing violence in our society, should I get a gun? I wish I had some real friends; I am not sure who I can trust. Then, if we are honest with ourselves, we see that our worst problems are not with what is going on with the world: they are with ourselves, our failings—yes, our sins.

Like an oasis in the wilderness, the bridal banquet brings peace and nourishment. As it renews the covenant between God and us, it also provides the basis of a relationship with others at the banquet. Of course, we are different people with a wide range of interests, affections, and even beliefs. But in this oasis, rivalries are put aside. Sin is forgiven. God has joined this group of sinners together as he feeds us with the bread and wine of the covenant, the body and blood of Christ.

Our Hero

A bridal banquet would be nothing without the anticipation of the marriage with the groom. What a guy! He is smart. Even as a child he amazed the scholars in the temple (Luke 2:46–47). When the religious heavyweights wanted to catch him on the rules, he went deeper to the moral heart of the matter (Mark 2:27–28). Later the political folks wanted him to choose sides between the Roman Empire and the Jewish resistance. He outsmarted them by telling them to both pay taxes and to give their whole lives to God (Matt 22:17–21).

Our guy also has courage. They told him that his ruler wanted to kill him. Jesus told them to tell that "fox" he was busy healing people and casting out real demons (Luke 11:32). He added that he knew death awaited him in Jerusalem. Never mind, he was going there. But he was not going without challenging the crooks who had taken over the temple, the people's most sacred place. With righteous anger he overturned the tables of the money changers, calling them "robbers." That sacred space was to be the house of prayer for all the nations (Mark 17:15–17).

Smart and courageous, yes, but in his heart, he is so compassionate. He cared about Peter's mother-in-law. She had a fever, and he cured her (Mark 1:30–31). Later he saw a leper, not good to look at and contagious as well. Jesus was moved with pity and healed him (Mark 1:40–42). Wherever he went he was met with the blind, crippled, demon-possessed, and he restored them to health. His compassion crossed political lines. He healed the slave of an enemy officer and praised him for his faith (Mark 1:5–13). Then as Jesus looked over the city of Jerusalem, he saw its coming destruction and wept for all those who would suffer and die. Coupled with being smart and courageous, he is loving and kind. What a guy! But does he love us? It is a question every bride asks herself, and in reverse, every groom as the wedding approaches.

Sharing in the Task

Marriage changes things. The focus of one's life is turned inside out from being concerned about "me" to being concerned about "us." At times, it may also mean giving up one's own ambitions and destinations and adopting those of the one you love. A soldier marries his sweetheart, and she moves with him across the globe from base to base. A mother who is a physician takes an important position, and her husband gladly takes care of the house and looks after the children. At this bridal banquet we look ahead to what changes need to be made so that this marriage with Christ might succeed. His is a magnificent mission, and as his partner, we get to help.

Jesus' mission was to announce the nearness of the kingdom of God and work to bring it about. The kingdom of God was the fulfillment of the promises of the prophets. Sins would be forgiven (Isa 1:18). The blind would see, the deaf would hear, and the lame would leap like a deer (Isa 35:5–6). There would be food and plenty (Jer 31:12). Even the desert will bring forth springs of water (Isa 35:7). Slaves and hostages would be freed (Isa 61:1). The weapons of war will be changed into tools for peace, and all will have homes and jobs as they sit under their own vine and fig trees (Mic 4:3–4). Then came the greatest promise of all: "He will swallow up death forever" (Isa 25:8). And as Jesus works to fulfill these promises, as his bride, we get to help.

How will the goals of Christ change our lives? As we attend the bridal banquet we might think of these things. Before the meal we often pray the Lord's Prayer. When we say, "Thy kingdom come," the groom's whole mission is there. Then we pray for forgiveness, and food for others as well as for ourselves. Our hearts also plead for the Father to deliver us from all of the evils of our world, the ways, the conflicts, and even the health concerns of our loved ones. In a deeper relationship with our spouse-to-be, it is something to think about as we attend this bridal banquet.

Chapter 2

The Guest List

THE GUEST LIST AT the first Lord's Supper was a diverse group of fellows, including a thief who was soon to betray Jesus. No doubt there were political differences between Simon the Zealot, a Jewish nationalist, and Matthew, the tax collector who had worked for the Romans. All had followed Jesus for a while but had not really absorbed much of what he taught them. While the Passover was familiar to them, they were not prepared for the communion Jesus introduced. While Christ's body and blood were an incredible gift, it was also a teaching moment. They were to repeat it in remembrance of Jesus. Even their idea of their own importance was challenged. A dispute arose as to who was the greatest among them. Would it be the impetuous Peter, young John, or Nathaniel, in whom there was no guile? Jesus then declares the greatest is not the guest at the table who is being served but the one who does the service, the serving woman or the slave (Luke 22:14–30).

Who should be on the guest list for a small group communion? Yes, it should be made up chiefly of those who have followed Jesus for a while. They should be as diverse as the populations from which they come. There will be political differences;

there are bound to be. The disputes might also be about which party has the most to offer society. Jesus' words echo as he reminds us that greatness does not depend upon respect and power but on humility and service. Will all the guests really understand the meaning and significance of the Lord's Supper? Did the disciples that first night? It was a tremendous gift but also a teaching time. The full meaning of that Supper, that communion, would be more fully understood in the months and years to follow. That would also involve the guest list.

Sinners

Eating and drinking were an important part of Jesus' ministry. In that society, as in our own, people judged you according to your associates and eating companions. That is why it was a scandal that Jesus ate with tax collectors and notable sinners (Matt 9:11). In the house of a Pharisee, as Jesus was eating, a woman came in and anointed his feet with perfume and dried it with her hair. Her sins, though many, were forgiven (Luke 7:37–39). When the prodigal son returned home after devouring his father's money on prostitutes, his father forgave him and rejoiced at his return with a fine dinner (Luke 15:30–32).

As Jesus ate and drank with sinners, Holy Communion is foremost a meal for the forgiveness of sinners. When Jesus passed around the cup he said, "This is my blood of the covenant, which is poured out for many for the forgiveness of sins" (Matt 26:28). Throughout history the Lord's Supper has always been seen as the assurance of the forgiveness of sins. In many traditions it is called a "sacrament." One definition of the Latin *sacramentum* is the money deposited waiting for a case to be decided, in other words, "a sure thing." Partaking of the Supper means receiving that forgiveness of sins that has been kept in reserve, just waiting for us.

But what if you find yourself "locked" into a sinful situation? What if you are addicted to drugs or alcohol? What if you are in a profession, like the tax collectors at the time of Christ, whose profession was connected with extortion? What if you have been trafficked for sex and cannot get out? Then one remembers the prostitutes Jesus dealt with in his ministry. Many of them had no place to go in that society with their reputation. Would Jesus still accept them, eat with them, forgive them? The woman, who was a sinner, and maybe could not change her life, wept and bathed Jesus' feet with her tears. With the anguish of repentance, forgiveness was assured for her and also for us in the days ahead.

Poor People Included

They celebrated the Lord's Supper in Corinth but made a mess of it. The well-off Christians got together and were duly served by slaves as was the custom at that time. It was at a regular meal, and some enjoyed the wine a bit too much. When the dishes were washed and put away the Christian slaves gathered with their masters for communion. But the wine was finished and some of the people were drunk. The slaves were humiliated. Though they were fellow Christians in the body of Christ, the way the Lord's Supper was practiced just reminded them that they did not belong. Christians though they may have been, they were still slaves.

Though it does not refer directly to the Lord's Supper, Jesus' parable of the wedding feast provides an interesting perspective to this account of the Supper. At the wedding feast, when the first to be invited made their excuses to miss out on the feast, the king sent his slaves to search out for the poor people on the streets to share in the banquet (Matt 22:9–10). Like the Corinthian account, Jesus' parable makes a special point of bringing together the rich and poor in a meal. When slaves were in the same house with their masters, together they communed with Christ, and together they found themselves knitted together as members of Christ's body. When the rich and the homeless are so widely divided in modern society, it might take some effort to bring them together in this bridal banquet for the king's Son.

Bringing together the rich and poor in emergency situations might actually be easier. Here one thinks of nongovernmental organization workers bringing food and medical supplies to refugee camps in the Middle East and Africa. From the organizers the call goes out to Christians in the camp and those bringing in the aid. We are having a meal together with the Lord's Supper. Come if you can and be part of our fellowship. Conversely, one of the refugees, an African pastor, asks the aid workers to supply the bread and wine for the Lord's table and invites them to participate.

With this understanding of the Lord's Supper, it can be a powerful tool in bringing together people that society has divided. Speaking about the fellowship at the Lord's table Paul writes, "Because there is one bread, we who are many are one body, for we all partake of the one bread. Consider the people of Israel; are not those who eat the sacrifices partners in the altar?" (1 Cor 10:17–18). If the Lord's Supper can bring together people from different classes, races, and nations, can it also bring together people from different churches, denominations, and traditions, as well as those who have never belonged to a church?

Communing Divided Christians

When Paul criticized the way the Corinthians celebrated the Lord's Supper, he did so because of the factions in the Corinthian congregation. He writes, "For, to begin with, when you come together as a church, I hear that there are divisions among you; and to some extent I believe it. Indeed, there have to be factions among you, for only so will it become clear who among you are genuine" (1 Cor 11:18–19). Earlier, Paul had complained, "For it has been reported to me by Chloe's people that there are quarrels among you, my brothers and sisters. What I mean is that each of you says, 'I belong to Paul,' or 'I belong to Apollos,' or 'I belong to Cephas,' or 'I belong to Christ'" (1 Cor 1:11–12). Communing together as one body in Christ put their unity in Christ above their divisions.

The present denominational system could learn from this teaching of Paul. However, if, for whatever reason, people are no longer as involved in the organized churches and their divisions, this emphasis of Paul is good news. Though Christians have come from different traditions, with even diverse views of the sacrament, their unity in Christ is more important, and in the Lord's Supper they can even learn from one another. In a beautiful conversation at the Supper people can talk freely about what wonderful gifts they have found in communing with Christ in the Lord's table.

Are there some limits as to who should come to the Lord's Supper? Must one be baptized? Should one be properly instructed as to the nature and purpose of the sacrament? Should children be of a certain age? Some organized churches have traditions and even rules about this and make participating in the sacred meal a reward for reaching an age or attending a class. Yet, a more natural way to invite people to the sacrament is simply to ask them if they want to receive Christ into their lives in this wondrous meal. If they are not sure they might simply fold their hands and receive a blessing. While most of the participants have probably been baptized, nowhere in the Scriptures is baptism considered to be necessary for receiving Christ in the Supper.

Enemies

The Jewish people at the time of Christ and the apostles had strong rules about eating with the unrighteous, which included tax collectors and sinners. This is why it was such a scandal that Jesus ate at the home of Matthew and Zacchaeus. However, those rules were even more pointed against eating with non-Jews. And if these were part of the Roman occupation, the enemy of the Jewish dream of a free nation, it would be even more appalling. To break down this barrier a Roman centurion, Cornelius, had a vision of an angel who told him to send for Peter. At the same time Peter had a vision commanding him to eat unclean food in preparation for the invitation Peter received to meet with the Roman (Acts 10:1–36). Later defending his actions, it turned out that Peter ate with the centurion, an enemy of the Jews (Acts 11:3). While this meal was not the Lord's Supper, it demonstrates in no uncertain terms that in Christ political barriers are overcome. If this is demonstrated in an ordinary meal, it is even more meaningful in the Holy Communion.

Communing with the enemy is most poignant when fellow Christians, who detest each other, gather at the Lord's Supper. They might be political opponents or family members going through marital difficulties. Here the Cornelius story has several applications. The first is that Cornelius was a good man, devout, generous, and a believer in God, though he did not know of Christ. Are our enemies good people in their own way? Peter summed it up in this way: "I truly understand that God shows no partiality, but in every nation anyone who fears him and does what is right is acceptable to him" (Acts 10:34–35). The second application is that it is sin that makes enemies and Christ died to take away sin. Then in this Holy Communion with Christ, sin is forgiven and reconciliation between God and human beings is confirmed. If this huge problem has been addressed then the reconciliation of enemies here is also possible and likely.

Reconciliation of enemies is also very important in refugee camps around the world. Uprooted by war and drought, people are thrown together who have had their lives threatened and even ruined by their political enemies. Now in the camp old realities are different even though resentment against old enemies lingers. Is there anything praiseworthy in these erstwhile opponents? If they come to the same worship service or Bible class, can we see them as fellow believers? As to sin, are we forgiven our enmity? Are they? Perhaps as we commune together the anger will go away, and the resentment will fade. Communing with the enemy will always be a wonderful blessing of the Eucharist.

On a personal level can you really commune with those with whom you have some profound disagreements and enmity? Christ's words here are most instructive: "So, when you are offering your gift at the altar, if you remember that your brother or sister has something against you, leave your gift there before the altar and go; first be reconciled to your brother or sister, and then come and offer your gift" (Matt 5:23–24).

The guest list for the bridal banquet is very large. You are bound to meet some new people. The nice thing is that you will have something in common with them. None of them are perfect.

All of them will be sinners, some will be poor. Maybe you can identify with them if you have been poor sometime during your life. Then there will be the strangers, people with different habits, customs, traditions, and sometimes, values. While these identities often separate us in the everyday world, we also have something else in common. We also have suffered pain in our lives. As we commune with all those people who are different from ourselves we do know that all of us have suffered, and that also binds us together in the Supper. Then, after having communed, maybe our attitude toward people who are different from us undergoes a change. Together we are a community of those who have sinned, been forgiven, and shared some of the pain which helps us understand and appreciate each other.

Chapter 3

The Menu

THE BRIDAL BANQUET FEATURES "comfort food." It is bread and wine, but it is comfort food because of the meaning and memory it brings. On the night he was betrayed, "Jesus took a bread, and after blessing it he broke it, gave it to the disciples, and said, 'Take, eat; this is my body.' Then he took a cup, and after giving thanks he gave it to them, saying, 'Drink from it, all of you; for this is my blood of the covenant, which is poured out for many for the forgiveness of sins'" (Matt 26:26–28).

Sometimes with comfort food it is hard to remember why that food is so soothing. Was it the memory of a date at a nice restaurant or a sandwich when we were half starved? It might have been a similar cut of beef, but it brings many layers of memories. Do we remember our first communion? Does the image of Da Vinci's painting of the Last Supper come to mind? Some might remember a pastor bringing a little wafer of bread and a sip of wine while we preparing to go in for surgery.

There are also deeper layers of meaning in our comfort food. What did Jesus mean when he said, "Take, eat; this is my body . . . this is my blood of the covenant?" The very idea of eating Christ's body and drinking his blood sounds bewildering if not offensive. Where in the world did that picture come from and in what way could it possibly be smoothing? To understand that language we can go back to the first Lord's Supper and understand its context.

Passover

Jesus and his disciples were celebrating the Passover. This was a meal to remember: the night when the angel of death would be killing the firstborn of every family in Egypt except for those who followed certain instructions. They were to kill a lamb without spot or blemish and take the blood of the Lamb and put it on the doorposts of their homes. They were also to make unleavened bread for their coming journey which would not mold during the long journey. As they ate of the Lamb and the unleavened bread they were saved from death. At the same time the whole people were liberated from slavery. Since that first night the Passover has been celebrated every year since by the Jewish community.

Jesus and his disciples were celebrating the Passover when he instituted the Supper. They had eaten the Lamb in memory of the first Passover. It was a look back at the liberation of the Jewish people and God's contribution to the lasting covenant with them. When Jesus instituted the new covenant he offered the unleavened bread as his body. He was the Lamb. He offered the wine as the blood on the doorposts which protected them from destruction. As the Passover looked back, the Lord's Supper looked forward. Christ would be the Lamb shedding his blood on the cross for the salvation of all. We then receive the assurance of that salvation as we eat his body in the bread and drink his blood in the wine. But even with that explanation, it is still a mystery, and Christians have disagreed over the centuries as to its meaning.

Receiving Christ

Some Christians just believe that in the Lord's Supper we receive Christ's real presence in the bread and wine without seeking to explain it. Others consider that it is necessary to believe a change has occurred in which there is no longer bread and wine but the body and blood of Christ.[1] Still others affirm the presence of Christ at the Eucharist but do not link that presence with the signs of bread and wine.[2] As someone once said, no one believes in the "real absence" of Christ at the Supper. Currently there has been a lot of mutual understanding of one another's view of the sacrament, leading to more intercommunion of people across denominational lines.[3] If this is true of organized churches, it is probably even more so in house churches and small group communions where people come from different traditions. Above all, in this bridal banquet, while tasting the bread and enjoying the good wine, we experience the groom's presence and are thrilled with his love.

The Most Expensive Meal

It is only natural that we check the menu to see what the items cost. Most often we go for the best meal at the lowest cost. But on a celebratory occasion we take the most expensive item we can find and relish it with joy. When Jesus told his disciples, "Do this in remembrance of me" (Luke 22:19), they were to remember Jesus' sacrifice of his blood in the creation of a new covenant between God and us. In terms of cost, no other item we might taste can compare with Jesus giving up his life for our sins and transgressions.

How shall we enjoy the best part of the meal? In some circumstances, like the at the deathbed of a man facing eternity, there will be just a bit of bread in a wafer and a sip of wine, so like what the Syrophoenician woman requested of Jesus, just what crumbs fall from the master's table (Matt 7:28). Yet at other

---

1. World Council of Churches, *Baptism, Eucharist, and Ministry*, 11.
2. World Council of Churches, *Baptism, Eucharist, and Ministry*, 10.
3. World Council of Churches, *Baptism, Eucharist, and Ministry*, 17.

times, especially in a house church, the best comes last. At the Passover, it was likely that Jesus passed about the bread and cup at the end of the meal, which included all the traditional Passover foods. Similarly, in a small group meeting in a home or a restaurant's private room, a regular meal might be served with communion reserved for the best part of the meal. In this case all that comes before that most expensive item on the menu might just be considered as "appetizers."

What Is In the Food?

In calorie-conscious societies, the menu sometimes tells you what is in the food. How many calories are there? The menu at the bridal banquet is right up front about that. Receiving Christ in the bread and wine, we are nourished with the forgiveness of sins. While listing calories in a menu is only important for those counting calories, the forgiveness of sins is really only important for those who are conscious and bothered by the sins they have committed. This is why in a church service communion is often preceded by the confession of sins.

True community is seldom found when, like the disciples, there is a debate about who is the greatest. Rather, true community comes through the humility that is revealed in a mutual confession of wrongdoing in thought, word, and deeds. A small house church might be the place where people might reveal the specifics of their sinful problem. Yet even a general confession without mentioning to the group a specific sin can be a humbling experience. When there is a mixed group of rich and poor people, a poor woman confesses her jealousy of those who do not have to worry about food and a rich man confesses his anger over being criticized and taxed because of his wealth.

Many Christians believe that they have forgiveness always, whenever they ask. Why is forgiveness in the Lord's Supper any different or better? Many Christians refer to the Lord's Supper as well as baptism as a "sacrament." As was mentioned previously, a Latin dictionary defines a sacrament as the money put aside in a court case before the trial to pay for any damages. In the "sacrament" of the Lord's Supper Christ's forgiveness has been deposited to pay for any sin we have committed. It provides the certainty of forgiveness; we can depend upon it in eating the bread and drinking the wine.

The Forever Meal

Eating the bread and drinking the wine, we remember the words of Jesus: " I am the bread of life." Referring to our deepest hunger for meaning, he continues, "Whoever comes to me will never be hungry, and whoever believes in me will never be thirsty" (John 6:35). Then, in dangerous situations, in a refugee camp, on a battlefield, or on our deathbed, Jesus comforts us. He declares, "I am the living bread that came down from heaven. Whoever eats of this bread will live forever" (John 6:51). Again, he said, "Those who eat my flesh and drink my blood have eternal life, and I will raise them up on the last day" (John 6:52).

The promise of eternity is not a sad and gloomy prospect; rather, it is coming home after some tough times. In the story of the prodigal son, the younger son has wasted his inheritance, sown some sinful oats, and just about starved to death. Yet on his return his waiting father not only forgives him but welcomes his return and says, "Let us eat and celebrate; for this son of mine was dead and is alive again; he was lost and is found!" (Luke 15:23). For father and son, it was a time of union, communion, and joyful celebration. Our bridal banquet can be no less.

Bread and Wine

When Jesus broke the bread at the first communion it was unleavened bread. It was unleavened so that it would keep for a long journey. This meant that there would be enough bread to keep up the strength of the travelers. While unleavened bread might be useful as a symbol of the first communion and of the bread used at the Passover, other bread might be substituted, but there should be enough to keep us resilient through what might well be a difficult future.

In God's covenant with his people some bread also had about it a divine aura. In Israel's tabernacle and later the temple, the most sacred place was the holy of holies. In that sanctuary was the "bread of the presence." Made of the finest flour (Lev 24:5–9), this was another sign of the covenant between God and his people. Twelve loaves were made representing the tribes of Israel. This "bread of the presence" was so holy that it could only be eaten by the priests. Bread in our communion service continues to be a sign of God's covenant with us. Our "bread of the presence" is Christ himself. However, there is a radical difference between the "bread of the presence" in the holy place. When Jesus died, the curtain in the temple was ripped apart. Now the bread of the presence is not only for the priests. Now all are invited to eat the bread, the bread of the presence of God among us and in us.

With the bread is the wine. Isaiah looked beyond the times of destruction to the time when God would be the refuge of the poor and needy, and there would be the finest wine (Isa 25:1–8). At the wedding at Cana Jesus turned the water into wine, and it was the finest the guests had tasted (John 2:10). It was the wine at the Passover meal that Jesus said was the new covenant of his blood. No sheep needed to be sacrificed. It was the blood of Christ, soon to be crucified, that was the new sign of the covenant. In that communion with God and each other all can partake of the blood of Christ in the finest wine.

Does the wine in communion need to be wine made from grapes? Need it be alcoholic? What about those who come from churches where they serve grape juice instead of wine? Missionaries in tropical countries wonder whether they will need to import expensive wine just to have communion. In tropical Africa, palm wine is readily available. Some believers in India have used coconut milk. As with the question of unleavened bread, the form of the bread or the question of the wine is not as important as the words of institution setting apart these elements as special that convey to us the body and blood of Christ. It is the word of God that makes the elements the presence of Christ in this holy Supper. If served at the end of a meal, these words separate the bread and wine from the other food at the table. If shared at a time of crisis, they mark not only the food and drink but also the special "time-out" from the stress and danger all around. Christ shares his love, his forgiveness, and his presence to all those gathered around this meal as part of this wondrous bridal banquet.

Chapter 4

The Host and Servers

This bridal banquet is not sponsored and paid for by the bride's family and friends. It is provided by the groom. The real host for the banquet is Jesus. He sent out the invitations, made up the menu, and offers the food and drink. As the host he welcomes all. He loves the churchgoers who have stuck with him over the years. But he has also invited some notable sinners, promising forgiveness and a new life. Then when the banquet hall was not full, he has bought in people from the highways and byways, the refugees in the camps in Kenya and Chad. The homeless in Portland, the truck drivers bringing supplies to the survivors of disasters and war. With so many people from so many different places, how can they all be served? With a limited numbers of pastors and priests, certainly many will need to wait for the food and the blessings of the banquet. If those professional clergy need to be paid, where will the money come from to be able to feed all these people with the bread of life? For the small house churches in China and Bangladesh, must they miss out on the banquet?

The early church in the Bible had a solution for this problem. In Acts 14:23 Paul blessed elders to lead the small communities.

These people came from the communities themselves, probably as volunteers. After that, whenever believers gathered together, they would have servers who would teach, baptize, and celebrate Holy Communion. We know that they had communion in Corinth. We can also assume they had it at Lydia's home in Philippi. No doubt Aquila and Priscilla celebrated it in Ephesus. Roland Allen writes of Paul, "He taught them the form of the administration and the meaning of the two sacraments of Baptism and the Lord's Supper. There is not a shadow of evidence that sacraments were considered optional in the early church."[1]

In his First Letter to Timothy, Paul lays out the qualifications of the elders (there called "bishops") for the churches (1 Tim 3:1–7). Here the chief emphasis is on moral qualities. Of the fifteen items there are eleven moral qualifications, one moral-intellectual, one of experience, and two concerned with reputation. In the second list in Titus 1:5–9 there is but one moral-intellectual qualification: holding to the faithful word.[2] With regard to leadership in the new churches Paul cautions Timothy not to lay hands hastily on those who are to be leaders and partake of other people's sins (1 Tim 5:22). Once again, the qualifications for leadership in the small communities were chiefly moral rather than academic. There were valuable teachers in the early church who guided the churches in doctrine and through visits and letters. However, local elders and other communion servers did not necessarily need a strong education. In our modern world, can far more people be servers at the bridal banquet so that more people can come?

Liberating Communion

Over the centuries the sacredness of Lord's Supper led people to erect barriers around it to preserve its value. Harkening back to the Old Testament sacrifices, those who served needed to be called "priests." Though Lydia probably celebrated communion in her

---

1. Allen, *Missionary Methods*, 116.
2. Allen, "Case for Voluntary Clergy," 139.

home, now only a man could be a priest. But could any man be a priest? Now some type of special education was required. At first it was probably "learning by doing" under supervision. Later, it would be through academics in a seminary or university. In time, bishops were no longer elders in small churches; now they were professionals governing many churches. The church could also limit attendance to communion to those who had received adequate instruction. While some of this instruction was just about what communion was, the instruction could be expanded to include knowledge of a whole catechism of Christian teaching. This teaching, no doubt, was good and valuable, but making it necessary for receiving the Lord's Supper subtly changed its meaning. Then attending the communion was often seen as a graduation ceremony for a good job well done.

The selection and training of those who should preside at the Lord's Supper has led to many of the evils of church control over the lives of its members. Whole hierarchies of church government have assumed that it was necessary to have a certified celebrant for the Lord's Supper. The medieval church placed whole regions under a ban that prevented priests from celebrating the Eucharist. Though the Protestant Reformation did away with papal control over the celebration of the Lord's Supper, most denominations still insisted that it was necessary to have an ordained clergyman to preside over the communion. Some church bodies even stipulated that unless people shared the same doctrinal beliefs as their denomination, they should not be allowed to participate. This has led to family divisions when husbands and wives cannot commune together because they come from different church bodies. Is it any wonder that newly planted churches avoid celebrating the Lord's Supper because it will just cause too much division among the people?

On reflection, all the restrictions on who shall celebrate the Lord's Supper are based upon man-made rules and not on the Holy Scriptures. As the early churches met together they gathered around a table at a meal and remembered Christ's sacrifice for their forgiveness and salvation. It was not complicated. If there was any requirement for their participation, it was that they were sinners. Since that includes all of us, the server only needs to assert that the presence of Christ in this bread and wine is for the forgiveness of sins. Yes, there is also a real communion of all those present. But the communion is not because they all agree on points of doctrine and life, but that they are all forgiven sinners.

Introducing the Servers

Who should be the servers at the Lord's table? At a regular church it will be the pastor or priest. But what if no pastor is available? If the community wishes to have communion they will often recognize a natural leader who is spiritually mature, is gifted with humility, and who knows how to repent. In line with the New Testament, it might either be a man or a woman. Depending on the community it might be an elder or a younger person. Many potential servers may be unaware of their potential to be servers of the Lord's Supper. Yet others will quickly recognize their suitability for such a rule.

Servers also need to be trained and equipped to share the Lord's Supper with others. It is not that hard. Some can simply copy what they have experienced. With a little coaching they can practice bringing the power of the word of God to the elements of bread and wine for the forgiveness of sins and power to lead a better life. As part of their preparation, they will also learn the awe that comes from being a vehicle of Christ's presence and grace in this meal. As good waiters at the Lord's table they should also be able to describe the meal to strangers who may not know the ingredients of the meal or the spiritual food value of what is coming. Some in attendance may not understand any of this, so the server might suggest that they skip this part of the meal until they have an appetite for it.

While any group of Christians can celebrate communion with their own servers, they do so as part of the entire church on earth. This connection between a small community and the whole body of Christ can be demonstrated through the blessings of other Christians. This is good practice in order to discourage a self-appointed server from taking over and dominating the group. In the days of Paul, the connection with the wider Christian community was through the laying on of hands. In a small church that is losing their pastor, one of his final tasks might be for the pastor to bless one or more elders to celebrate the Lord's Supper. As a member of the church is going to a place where there is no church, several Christians, or perhaps a pastor, might bless him/her for communion services to be held where there is no church. And in some rare cases where a community arises without contact with the wider Christian world, the gathered people might simply bless one or more of their leaders to celebrate the Supper based upon what they have learned from the Scriptures.

Introducing Change

It is one thing to introduce new servers to the celebration of the Lord's Supper. However, it may also be necessary to prepare all the communicants for what they might see as changes to the Supper with the new servers. For those educated to believe that only a priest or pastor might consecrate the elements, having a truck driver or mother of three do the same thing might be quite a shock. This, obviously, might need some attention and a bit of education. Here the Scriptures rather than a catechism or doctrinal text might be the best lesson book. A Bible study on the words of institution, the practice of the early church, and the situation at Corinth in 1 Cor 11:17–34 would be a good way of introducing the way in which the early church celebrated communion. There they will see how the practice of the Lord's Supper provided the freedom of the church to spread quickly at that time and ours. However, it will also demonstrate the dangers of misusing the Lord's Supper to create division rather than unity among God's people.

    Both server and participants are likely to come from diverse traditions and church bodies. This means that all might need to be introduced to fellow Christians whose backgrounds are quite different from theirs. While this might be a bit frightening to some, it can also be a joyous occasion and an answer to all their prayers for the unity of the church. Among strangers, an important part of any communion service might be for people to introduce themselves, their background, and why they want to receive communion. Some might admit ignorance of their own religious beliefs and simply ask questions of others. This presents a wonderful opportunity to witness one's faith and beliefs concerning the forgiveness of sins in the Lord's Supper.

Theological Education

One of the chief reasons why celebrating the Lord's Supper has been reserved for pastors and priests is to make sure that the whole church might benefit from a good theological education. However, for the most part, in the modern world, it is assumed that this happens in a seminary or the divinity department of a university. Traditionally, this meant that future pastors needed to know or become familiar with the original languages of the Bible, Hebrew and Greek. However laudable this was for biblical scholarship, it effectively washed out a number of students who would have made fine pastors but could not handle the languages. Biblical doctrinal, historical, and practical subjects came next, often taught by experts in those areas who may or may not have had the personal skills needed for ministry. Good students were those who did well in academics. Others were graduated hoping that "at least" they would be good at ministering to the people in parishes.

Those communing at the Lord's table need more theological education, not less. Yet the New Testament is instructive on how this might be done. Learning more about God's word and will did not come from knowing most of the answers before problems emerged. Rather, it came from addressing the issues that were arising from within the community. Might gentiles, unfamiliar with the history, traditions, and Bible of the Jews, be admitted into the Christian fellowship? The Council of Jerusalem, and the Letters to the Galatians and Romans, were written to address this dispute. Was Jesus' resurrection real and will we be raised? Paul addresses this in 1 Cor 15.

Many theological issues will arise within a community gathered around the word and the Lord's table. Others will come from the confrontation of the gospel with the world all around. Many of these debates can be handled within the gathered community. Still others might well require some expertise from a contemporary St. Paul, well equipped to condemn falsehood, underscore the truth, and able to gave some old-fashioned advice. With modern technology, such answers need not wait for a letter to come slowly by land and sea. Rather, once trust is established between the people and a teacher, communication can be nearly instantaneous.

In an established church, there may be no need for lay people to act as servers and celebrants of the Lord's Supper. However, when clergy are no longer available for frequent celebrations, when a new small mission group is formed, when aid workers are far from home serving the vulnerable, when a house church is contemplating their first communion, God's "lay people" can certainly be blessed to preside and serve holy communion.

Chapter 5

The Banquet Hall

No, it does not need to be a "hall." For regular churchgoers now without a pastor, it will continue to be the small church from where their folks were buried, and some were married. In that familiar setting several of the elders will continue to use the service with which all the people are familiar. However, if the number of members shrinks to just a few, going through the whole service might feel a bit uncomfortable, not quite fitting for the remaining five people who still gathered. "What if we met at my home?" invited one. "Could we combine it with a meal?" suggested another. "We could all bring something to eat and then have a little service."

In a small town with a lot of vacant stores and houses, the most popular eating place was still Joe's Restaurant. A lot of the old-timers could nurse a cup of coffee for the time it took to discuss the day's events and the problems the community was having. Then the conversation turned to the fact that the Methodist church was closing its doors like another church had done last year. "Yeah, all the kids are leaving, and after COVID, they just could not put it all back together. It looks like they are going to sell the church, and the elevator is going to use it for storage. Hey,

Joe, what if we had church in your back room? We could invite all those who do not want to drive another twenty-five miles to go to their own church someplace else. Mike, weren't you one of the elders at the Methodist church? Maybe we could put something together. I heard about a restaurant church in another community. Maybe we could pull that off here."

At the Soup Kitchen

Unlike the houses in Corinth, most of the poor (slaves) no longer live on our premises. Seldom do we see those who sleep in the tents on our streets come to the church for communion. Church folk sometimes serve at soup kitchens on Thanksgiving and Christmas. It is nourishing food and very worthwhile, but something is missing. Often there is little real communion between those who give and those who receive. At communion in church, people feel a bond, however fragile, with others at the table. All are sinners; all saved by Christ. We are bound together by his grace. But are we at one with those whose lives have been fractured and deformed? Many of them daily help each other survive in a dangerous environment. Some of them are often effusive about their faith, even as we may be shy about ours. What if before the meal we said that all those who wished to share in communion might stay? The servers would say a few words about how partaking of this bread and wine is receiving Christ for the forgiveness of our sins and how we are all the body of Christ. Then before we all return to our homes, wrecked RVs, and tents we know we have been communing with Christ and his people.

And then what? While it might be difficult to remember a communion service at church two months ago, the service at the soup kitchen sticks in the mind and in the soul. The tent dweller goes home not only with a full stomach but a connection, thin though it may be, with those other folks. Maybe they learned something; maybe I did too. All that religious stuff, maybe some of it is real. Maybe there is hope. To all the servers the communion was almost surreal. Sharing the bread and wine in that place with those people continues to raise questions. Is there more we can do about these our fellow communicants? Should we do it more often? If we are all the body of Christ, how can I help? How can they help me?

The Retirement Home

Some of the residents have been there for several years. There is a Bible class, sometimes taught by one of the residents and other times by a pastor of a local church. On Sunday morning there is a broadcast from a local community church so some of the residents feel like they have been to church. Still, there is no opportunity for the Lord's Supper. One of the residents had a health setback. If she still had any connection with a local church the pastor or priest would come with communion. But many residents had come from another town or state and had never made any connections with a local congregation. A local pastor wondered whether he might offer communion, but would that only be for members of his denomination? If he invited others, would they feel like outsiders?

A staff member who felt responsible for some of those having a tough time thought that the idea of a communion service would be a good idea. She talked to others on the staff and to a few members of the community she thought might be interested. In the meeting room they used for presentations, exercises, and bingo on Tuesday mornings, they decided to ask people if they would like a brief service with communion. About seven said that they were interested. Before they had a service they talked about what each of them thought of communion. The answers were varied, but they all thought that it would be helpful. The staff member read from the Bible the words of institution and the account in 1 Corinthians. A simple service was prepared and all communed.

The Bigger Tent

The refugee camp was a virtual city of tents for well over 600,000 people. But one near the entrance of the camp was bigger. It was a meeting place for those responsible for the camp. They were looking for a more permanent building but all they had so far was this bigger tent. They were from the United Nations High Commissioner for Refugee Agency and from the World Food Organization, together with those in charge of security and housing. Occasionally they were joined by the truck drivers bringing in food and supplies. Most had their own tents to stay in, but this was their meeting place. It was a busy place with refugees coming in daily with requests and demands that could not always be met.

Now more refugees were arriving and there was simply no place to put them. Tempers shortened; tears were shed. Word came that the food trucks would be delayed. The money for food from across the world was running out. Many of the staff were thinking of quitting. "Where do we get the power to stay here and stick it out?" One of the staff, a former priest, no longer recognized or active, knew that this was a call for God's help, for the strength communion can bring to a troubled situation. Would anyone be interested in an ecumenical communion service, even led by an unrecognized priest? That Sunday staff, truck drivers, and a few interested refugees met in the bigger tent to receive Christ for forgiveness and the determination to stick it out and help as best they could. It was the bridal banquet hall in that place.

Carol's House

They originally met at the faculty wives' club. That was a group that operated a little storehouse of old furniture for foreign students and their wives. The group at Carol's house, however, had gotten close to each other. Their kids attended the same schools, and they all liked to gather to do some stitching and just enjoy one another's company. They loved to talk about university policies, the state of the nation, what they were planning for Christmas, and the best movie they had seen. They even talked about religion. Most of them used to attend church but they had stopped attending. They had come from different denominations and most, if pressed, would admit to praying now and then. Once the question came up, "Do you miss church?" "Not really," most said. One, however, said that she really missed communion. It was a real spiritual blessing, and she used to feel close to the others communing, "Sort of like I feel it here with all of you."

"Could we have it here?" said another. I once heard one of the university chaplains talking about the possibility and potential of house churches in the university community. He said he did not have the time to be at every one, but he would be happy to help begin some if they would provide the leadership to continue. "Maybe we could just do it around a meal or coffee. It is kind of a leap but if we all agree, maybe we should try." After six months of having an occasional communion service at Carol's house, they invited those husbands who were interested in finding out what their wives were doing. One of them said, "This is really a sneaky way of getting us to think again about what we really believe."

Retreat Center at Pune

It was a small meeting of Christ Bhaktas at Pune, India. Some of them were known previously at "unbaptized believers." After some presentations a leader arose and suggested that they celebrate *prasad*, which in Hindu culture was that which is offered to a god and distributed as a blessing to the people. The leader, known in Hindu culture as a *Sannyasin*, one who has devoted his life to spiritual things, explained that they would be celebrating communion within the Hindu culture. Christ Bhaktas, many from the upper castes in Hindu society, believe in Christ as the only path to salvation. However, they are not part of any organized Christian church.

Gathering around an oil lamp with many wicks, the leader took a coconut in his hand and with a machete broke it open. As the coconut milk ran down his hand into a basin he said, "Christ was broken for our sin, and with his blood we are saved." He then blessed the milk in the basin, and with a plate of cut bananas, he introduced the body and blood of Christ for our salvation and our community. Reverently the elements were passed about for all those present; later a voice was heard saying, "Jesus has finally come to us in our culture."

Crow Creek

It was quite an occasion in the Alaskan Native American village. An Episcopalian priest had come to say goodbye. He would not be able to come anymore; there were not enough priests. But all was not lost. He encouraged the small church to continue to worship with a lay preacher who had been helping out. He and one of the village elders said that they would continue to hold services and asked the priest if they could also celebrate Holy Communion. It was not ordinarily OK, but this would be a "permanent" emergency. "Sure," he said and asked the two to come forward. He laid his hands on them and blessed them for their ministry at Crow Creek.

Would they know how to do communion right? The elder mused that he did not know how to do all this church stuff, but he knew ritual. He had been doing it for many years as one of the wise men of the community. It was different but like some of the native stuff. It brought people together; it got them in tune with the divine. Might it get infused with some native practices? He wondered how the Lord's Supper got from being a nice meal to little wafers and a sip of wine. Is this how those white folks changed the Supper to fit their church culture? Hmm.

A House Church Near You

Their disagreement with their pastor and the church was pretty profound. Yes, they were still believers, but their church, as they saw it, was neither true to the faith, nor was it meeting their needs. On a hunch, Jill looked online for a house church. There it was in bold letters: "Find a house church near you." It was part of an international group of house churches. She was intrigued, and the couple talked about it. "Should we find out?" A few emails and phone calls made the connections, and they cringed a bit as they decided to join but were warmly welcomed.

Everyone was invited to introduce themselves and many talked about why they were here. They had come from different denominations but said how much they enjoyed this type of fellowship. They sat down for meal and had a wonderful discussion on what the Bible lesson had to say for their lives. They then closed the meal with Holy Communion served by the hostess that evening. Coming back home, Jill and her husband talked about their experience. "It sure was different, but I kind of liked it," he said. "Do you think we will fit in?" she replied. After talking about it they agreed they would go back.

The Prophetic Community

They met at a march protesting the cuts to the Agency for International Development and its possible closure. Some of them had served overseas for the agency working with hunger relief. Others had been in the Peace Corps and knew firsthand the benefits to the people that had come from the agency. They were joined by an old missionary who had served in Nigeria. At his invitation, the marchers had assembled at his church before hitting the street. Not a stunning success; they agreed to recruit even more protesters on the coming Saturday. More showed up and the demonstration received some national news. The newscaster admitted that foreign aid was a low priority for most Americans, but that was not true for those who knew its importance in the lives of the people they knew overseas.

The missionary invited some of the most passionate advocates to come back and meet once a month on Wednesday evenings. About eight showed up and the missionary began with prayer. How do we keep going against an administration and even a society that does not seem to care about what is happening in our world? Discouraged, some stopped coming. Others asked the old missionary what they should do. He told them about a couple working for the Agency for International Development (AID) in Africa who were so discouraged they asked him to have a communion service with them. The bond that was made, the encouragement of Christ at the table at that time, said something to the group. "In the here and now maybe we should have communion just to keep going."

"Amen to that," said the old missionary. "We will start next time we meet."

The halls for the bridal banquet can really be different, from a formal church to a soup kitchen, a Native American village or a retreat in India. Yet as they welcome people to receive Christ in the Supper and to commune with fellow sinners, those halls take on a beauty and dignity they did not have before. That is where they meet Jesus again, and that made all the difference.

All these banquet halls are different but are probably similar to places for communion in the early church. For those who have communed in a certain place for much of their lives, that place, often a church sanctuary, is deeply embedded in their consciousness as a holy place, a place where they had the opportunity to be with Christ in the Lord's Supper. Yet, for some of us who have experienced communion meals in far-off places, in strange surroundings, those places too have taken on a spiritual memory which we will not forget. A missionary coming away from a nation in conflict gathered in a rundown hotel with people from many backgrounds who were also fleeing. Someone proposed a communion service, and there at a scarred table with rickety chairs, missionaries from different denominations, government officials, a barmaid at the hotel, and some frightened tourists communed together. As they went their way that hotel left a mark on their memory as the place where God had brought them all together that time as one body in Christ.

Chapter 6

Banquet Gifts

AT AN ELABORATE BANQUET you can expect some gifts for those who attend. Given that our host is the image of the invisible God, the firstborn of all creation, the gifts are not trivial little souvenirs that are soon thrown away. Since he was fully human he understands our needs and gives us gifts we will value and use. Because of his generosity, there is not just one little gift next to the plate. Instead, there is a package, carefully wrapped, containing as many as eight jewels, each worth a fortune.

The Ruby—The Forgiveness of Sins

The forgiveness of sins is the chief gift from the Lord's Supper. In Matthew, Jesus said, "This is my blood of the covenant which I poured out for many for the forgiveness of sins" (Matt 26:28). For those going to communion every Sunday, the gift is the forgiveness of sins of last week, the anger over an argument, and injuring a friend with a biting comment. For those whose attendance is infrequent there is often such a long list of sins that it is impossible to even remember them. Sometimes the offense is a big one that keeps you up at night. Unfaithfulness to a spouse, a divorce, an auto accident you caused, the words you uttered that have permanently ruined a family relationship—all forgiven.

The forgiveness is part of the covenant Jesus spoke about. He is our God, and we are his people. Like the father forgave the prodigal son after he had wasted his inheritance because he loved his son, in holy communion God renews his covenant, his family relationship with us. And of course, there is the forgiveness of sins. It is constant and has the long life and the beauty of a ruby. Yes, and the color is the reminder that the forgiveness comes from the red blood of Christ. How much is it worth? It is a priceless gift we treasure and one which makes us want to return to the bridal banquet.

The Opal—The Gift of Community

Opals are unique. They are not all of one color; some are predominantly white, others black, but all contain a variety of hues. Yet, they are all within one jewel. As the stone is turned the different colors come through creating an enchanting whole. That is how a group of communicants must look like to God. Ginger, the new mother, carries her babe. Oscar, the judge, kneels next to her. There is Yung from China next to Devon, the punk rock fan. In this community there are farmers, shopkeepers, a physician, and three eighth graders. Just think to what sins they confessed; imagine what life will hold for them this next week. Yet, here they are together, one body of Christ.

If this is a wonder in a local gathering, think what it is like in the YMCA hostel in Hong Kong where some Christians from around the world have come as tourists, businessmen, designers, and government officials. Prayer was announced for eight in the morning, and communion was offered for those who were interested. Before they began they were to introduce themselves. A Ghanian, two from Shanghai, a British diplomat, a German engineer on his way inland, and a variety of soccer players greeted each other. From the ends of the earth God's children came together as a single community in the Lord's Supper. Nationalities are submerged for a time as God makes them a single people, unified for a moment, and with a memory of a time when all are one in Christ.

The Diamond—Reconciliation

The husband and wife always wanted to commune next to each other. They remembered that one time in their lives that they almost divorced, but when they reconciled, they communed with each other. It left a memorable impression on both of them which they have repeated now a thousand times since. Some conflicts are bigger than personalities. In the Corinthian congregation arguments arose about which of the leaders to follow. Should it be Paul, or Apollos, or Peter, or Christ (1 Cor 1:12)? Today some would ask, "Should it be Lutherans, or Methodists, or Roman Catholics, or evangelical nationalists?" Tragically these disputes have kept Christians from communing with each other for centuries. Some of the debate has been about how Christians understand what Paul meant when he said, "For all who eat and drink without discerning the body, eat and drink judgment against themselves" (1 Cor 11:29). Theologians have debated about how the bread is the body of Christ, but many have missed its singular, most obvious meaning. The people are the body of Christ. Regardless of traditions, denominations, or church identities, together they commune, one body, reconciled in Jesus Christ.

But there was another problem, referred to previously. What about the difference between the served and the servers, the rich and the poor, the masters and the slaves? In nations today, some of the greatest differences are not between Christian faiths as much as it is between political polarization. Can you be at one with those whose political persuasion you hate? Here Paul's castigation of the Corinthian communion is right on. You simply do not just celebrate the Lord's Supper with people of your own class and leave out those who are poor but share your faith. Shall we change the banquet hall to be more inclusive? Is there a better way to be reconciled with fellow Christians who are so different from us? Real reconciliation at the Lord's table will be one of the hardest issues we face. Only the hardness, beauty, and price of a diamond will do.

The Onyx—Emergencies

The black onyx is a symbol of strength in tough times; so is the Lord's Supper. Jesus celebrated with his disciples shortly before his crucifixion and death. Ever since those facing the threat of death and death itself have hungered for the seal of salvation, communion with our Lord. This is why people who are in the last days of their lives request Holy Communion. With that seal of forgiveness which one can taste and drink, people can die in peace. All the painful relationships are past, the problems are gone, and a better life awaits. During the COVID pandemic, pastors and priests were often not allowed to see their dying members. Thank goodness some nurses took the opportunity to serve those dying with communion.

There are other emergencies. Soldiers gather around to partake of communion before going into battle. They are frightened but comforted. They are in this together with their companions and with Christ. If they live, they live unto the Lord, and if they die, they die unto the Lord. Whether they live or die, they are the Lord's (Rom 14:8). There has been an earthquake, and a team has been assembled to see if they can find any survivors. More aftershocks are expected. Gone from home for weeks in a dangerous place, how does one prepare the spirit? A chaplain in the group has done this before. They kneel for communion. Now they are ready.

The Sapphire—Resilience for a Long Journey

The Passover which Jesus observed with his disciples used unleavened bread. That had been observed through the centuries and is still used today in the Jewish Passover and in many Christian communion services. It was unleavened so that it would last through the tough times ahead. Another gift of communion is that it provides patience and resilience for long periods of disruption, trial, and pain. How does one meet the realization that you have an incurable illness that leaves you in pain for the rest of your life? How does a mother cope with the birth of a child who will be permanently disabled? Where will an aid worker get the strength to continue when she finds out that there will be more refugees and less food to feed them?

At the Last Supper, Jesus and his disciples had more than one glass of wine. That too was a gift for resilience. It is probably why the disciples were too sleepy to watch with Jesus as he prayed in Gethsemane. Yet even a sip of wine reminds those partaking that there are breaks in suffering, bits of peace and joy even in the most difficult of journeys. But it is more than bread and wine. It is Christ in the bread who brings his lasting nourishment when we face a bleak future, and it is Christ in the wine who brings us joy, hope, and light in the gloom and darkness we often experience.

The Emerald—The Altar Call

Not everyone in a house church or a tent in a refugee camp is a Christian. Should communion be celebrated when one or more people, sometimes friends, are not Christian and really have not understanding of what communion is or what it might mean? In the communion service, that should be addressed, reminding all the meaning of communion and its gifts to our lives. In some churches there is an altar call, asking people to come forward to receive Christ into their lives. Inviting people to Holy Communion gives people another chance to receive Christ into their lives in partaking of Christ in the bread and wine. "If you wish to receive Christ for the forgiveness of sins, come join us in this celebration," might be an invitation. However, that might be followed by the statement, "If not, we are pleased that you are here."

For most Christians the Lord's Supper is a "means of grace" as people remember Christ's sacrifice or as people partake of the body and blood of Christ. Communion, thus, is not a gift for those who have been good, those who know a lot about the faith, or those who have decided for Christ. It is rather those who wish to receive Christ and his blessings at this time in their lives. Then through his communion with Christ and fellow believers the seed of faith is planted. Thus, this communion is a means of God's grace in Christ. It is interesting that some believe an emerald symbolizes mercy, compassion, and universal love. Maybe that is a fitting symbol of inviting others to see in Christ his mercy, compassion, and universal love.

The Agate—Starting Over

Agates are sometimes found on a beach. One of the memorable meals in the Bible was a breakfast on the beach of Lake Galilee. There, after his resurrection, Jesus had prepared a meal for Peter and the other fishermen. At his advice they had caught a large mess of fish. After the meal Jesus asked Peter three times whether Peter loved him. This duplicated the three times that Peter had denied his Lord. Each time Peter painfully replied, "Yes, you know that I love you." At this meal Jesus was inviting Peter to start all over again. It was an invitation now to live his faith and devotion after actually denying that he was even one of Jesus' followers.

One of the finest gifts of the Lord's Supper is that it gives us an opportunity to start over. There have been many opportunities to deny that we are followers of Jesus. Sometimes it has been years since we have been in any faithful relationship with him, then at the Lord's Supper we are invited to start over again, to renew that relationship with Christ. There we are forgiven our denial and our absence. After that meal Peter was given his mission and we are given ours. Now, how do we take the love that Jesus has shown us and share it with those around us? What changes might we make in our lives to say with Peter, "Yes, Lord, you know that I love you?"

Amber—For the Spiritually Tired

Communion is also for those who are too tired to remember their sins and too puzzled as to how to improve their lives. That is when we come trusting that God can do something with us when are not sure. Then we simply trust Christ to take us and enfold us with his grace and goodness. We are like the tiny insect caught in tree sap that through the ages has become petrified into beautiful amber. That little bug cannot move, cannot complain, cannot do anything to save itself. It is just embraced and held by the golden amber of God's eternal love. While all amber is beautiful, the most prized are those pieces that hold what once was dead but now is displayed as a witness to God's grace.

Amber is not only valued for its beauty and decorate art. It is also used by scientists as a witness to the history of trees and fossils. Having put ourselves completely into God's hands, his sticky tree sap, his eternal love, we too become witnesses of our God who communes with us when we were too tired to think, too weak to help ourselves, but simply to let his grace surround us. Then we become examples to others who are also spiritually tired as we invite them to commune with us.

The Pearl—Foretaste of the Feast to Come

The real pearl of great price at the Lord's table is the knowledge that no matter how elaborate or simple the meal, it is only an appetizer of the life to come. At the first communion Jesus said, "I will never drink of this fruit of the vine until that day when I will drink it new with you in my Father's kingdom" (Matt 26:29). Jesus knew what was ahead of him in terms of scorning, mockery, pain, and death. Yet he saw through that misery to see a marvelous meal in the kingdom to come. For many of us death is something we do not like to think about. In the midst of a busy life the thought of death is too depressing to think about. Yet it awaits all of us.

Here in the Lord's Supper our whole perspective of death is transformed. Here we are joined with Christ who said, "I am the resurrection and the life. Those who believe in me, even though they die, will live, and everyone who lives and believes in me will never die" (John 11:25–26). It is because of this hope that many who are about to die wish to receive communion. Then they are reminded that this meal is just a foretaste, an appetizer of what they will receive when they are with Christ in the life to come. The Lord's Supper is truly a pearl of great price. These are the bridegroom's gifts to all who attend the bridal banquet. They are real jewels, each one glowing at various times in our lives but all showing the generosity of the bridegroom who wants to make us his own.

Chapter 7

Sharing the Meal

SOME HOUSE CHURCHES AND other small groups share a common worship tradition. Baptists celebrate the Lord's Supper in one way, and Anglicans do it quite differently. In these situations, the following suggestions for a worshipful communion might be unnecessary. However, when people come together from different traditions, or the group is so small that a traditional liturgy seems unwieldy, the following might be useful.

A House Church Communion

A small group gathers to celebrate the Lord's Supper. It may be at the conclusion of a regular meal or a special communion service. Sometimes people know each other; at other times it is a meeting of strangers or a combination of the two. All who are present know that they are about to partake of the Lord's Supper. Before the meal or the time of communion the following program may be used with parts for the host and a helper. Maybe it might start with a song or hymn that is known by many.

The Beginning:

Helper: Why is this meal different from others?

Leader: In this meal we remember that Jesus Christ died and rose again for the forgiveness of sins and for our salvation. In this meal he offers his body and blood in the bread and wine as a covenant between God and us. As we eat this bread and drink this wine we are going to receive Christ in our bodies, minds, and hearts .

Helper: Let us not commune as strangers but as friends. Please tell us something about yourself. If you are new to this group can you tell us why you are here?

All: *Group discussion*

Hunger and Thirst:

Leader: We come from many different places. We have different interests and may hold some opposing values and beliefs. Yet we all have something in common. We are hungry and thirsty for wholeness. Perhaps it is for community, reconciliation with others, for a new start, for endurance in suffering, for courage to meet our own death. Many of our problems come from sin, our sin and those of others. We hunger and thirst for forgiveness.

All: Lord, we confess that we have sinned against you and against others. For the sake of your Son, Jesus Christ, forgive us and help us to do better.

Leader: We also have this in common: through Christ, God has forgiven our sins, and through his grace brings us wholeness, peace, and the energy to do his will.

Lesson from the Scripture:

Helper: *He reads one or more lessons from the Bible.*

All: *The group shares with each other what this passage says to them in their lives. If there are teachers of the Scripture present they may be called upon to share their insights and advice.*

Prayers:

Helper: *Leads with an opening prayer and invites people in the group to contribute with their own prayers.*

All: *Join in with their prayers.*

Helper: *Concludes the prayer time by inviting all to join in the Lord's Prayer.*

Communion:

Leader: In Holy Communion we receive Christ in the bread and wine, and Christ renews the covenant he made with us when he died for us on the cross. In this meal we have the assurance of forgiveness and a sense of community with our fellow believers. In this meal we are reconciled with God and with each other, and recognize that we are the body of Christ in this world. We are also strengthened in times of trouble and inspired to lead a better life. Now we can meet death unafraid, for we have the promise and certainty of heaven.

You are all invited to partake. If you are not a Christian but wish to receive Christ and his forgiveness in the bread and wine, we invite you to join us. If you are not sure at this time you may fold your hands and be blessed by our fellowship.

Leader: *Taking the bread the host says,* Our Lord Jesus Christ, the same night in which he was betrayed, took bread, and when he had given thanks, broke it and give it to his disciples, and said, "Take eat; this is my body, which is given for you. This do in remembrance of me."

Taking the wine the host says, "In the same way, he took the cup after supper, and when he had given thanks, he gave it to them, saying, "Drink of it, all of you; this cup is the new covenant in my blood which is shed for you for the forgiveness of sins. This do as often as you drink, in remembrance of me."

The bread and wine are passed around with the words, "The body of Christ for you," and "The blood of Christ shed for you." After they are finished the bread and wine are returned to the host.

Helper: We thank you, dear heavenly Father, for this gift of forgiveness, of fellowship, and salvation which you have given us in this bread and wine. May this keep us steadfast in the faith and strengthened to lead a godly life until we meet with you in the life to come. In Jesus' name we pray.

Leader: May the Lord bless us and keep us in these coming days and give us the strength to meet the challenges you set before us. Teach us more about your love and your will for us in our lives.

All: Amen

The group may conclude with another song or hymn, conversations leading to a closer friendships, and discussion about possible meetings in the future.

A Family Communion in Challenging Times

This is a service for a family in tough times like an epidemic when going to church is discouraged, or when an immigrant family fears deportation, or a conflict in the area that makes going out of the house dangerous. It may even be suitable when a member of the family will be undergoing surgery or facing death.

Preparation:

Leader: We begin this meal of thanksgiving in the name of the Father, the Son, and the Holy Spirit.

Our Father, we thank you for life and love, for joys and sorrows, for our family. For help in these times, and for your unfailing mercy. Now, in our sinful world, we face trouble in our lives. In these tragedies and in our daily life we confess our sinfulness, our selfishness that often rejoices in our good fortunes while forgetting the pain of others, some of which makes our good life possible. Forgive us, Father, and give us the wisdom and strength to make things better.

Response: Forgive us, Lord.

Leader: Through Jesus, God richly forgives us our sins and brings us together in love as his family.

Lesson from the Scripture:

Leader: Hear the lesson(s) for the day:

Response: *Discussion of the lesson*

The Prayers:

Leader: Father, we thank you for joining us into the one body of Christ and pray for the pastors and people of our congregation who are gathered in many different places during this time of need. We also pray:

For those with special needs whom we name in our hearts.

For those who are in danger of death and those who are fatally ill in this time of crisis.

For the unemployed and all who are struggling to cope with hunger and rent in this time of need.

For doctors, nurses, first responders, and essential workers that can keep them safe.

For politicians and government leaders, that they make wise decisions to keep their people safe.

Lord, in your mercy,

Response: Hear our prayer.

The Meal:

Leader: The first Passover was celebrated by families, and the first communion was in an upper room with friends. The early church also received its blessings in homes. Here, in this place, in this meal, we remember what Christ has done for us in our salvation. We also recall that in this meal, this mystery, Christ gives us his body and blood in our everyday bread and wine. In this communion we are not alone but are joined with fellow members of our congregation and with believers throughout the world in the whole body of Christ.

Our Lord Jesus Christ, on the night he was betrayed, took bread, and when he had given thanks, he broke it and gave it to his disciples, saying, "Take, eat, this is my body, which is given for you. This do in remembrance of me."

In the same way, he also took the cup after supper, and when he had given thanks, he gave it to them, saying, "Drink of it, all of you. This is the new covenant in my blood, which is shed for you for the forgiveness of sins; this do as often as you drink it in remembrance of me."

Sharing the Bread and Cup:

They offer each other the bread and wine, saying, "Take, eat, the body of Christ.—Take, drink, the blood of Christ."

Blessing:

Leader: May the body and blood of our Lord Jesus Christ strengthen and preserve us in body and soul unto life everlasting. Thank you, Lord, for giving us of yourself in this holy meal. Refresh our faith and inspire us to love our neighbors in this time of uncertainty and need. In Jesus' name we pray.

Response: Amen.

A Prophetic Community Communion

Many congregations cannot take strong prophetic stands against racism, climate change, persecution of immigrants, economic inequality, inadequate healthcare, and war. Some of this might offend those who support the church. Should those supporters stop or limit their contributions, the entire ministry of the church, including the celebration of the Lord's Supper, would be threatened. However, if both the sharing of the word of God and communion might be done in a small group setting without the need for financial support, a far more robust call for reform, generous contributions, and acts of service might take place.

Though there are many causes, prophetic communities might concentrate on working toward fulfillment of the promises of God in the prophets. Through those prophets God promised forgiveness, food, water, health and healing, liberation, home and jobs, the end of war and death. In his ministry Jesus brought forgiveness, healing, food, and the resurrection of the dead. He also warned the rich, praised an oppressor for his faith, and commended aliens for their trust and kindness.

This communion service is for a group that has come together and desires to be fed and energized at this communion service. If there are strangers in the group all should introduce themselves and their curiosity or interest in this communion service.

Beginning:

Leader: We begin in the name of our God, our Father, who has created all people to be of equal importance; our Lord Jesus Christ, who healed, fed, forgave, and was especially kind to the poor and despised; and the Holy Spirit, who continues to inspire us to believe, love, help, and support all those in need.

Response: Help us, good Lord.

Confession and Forgiveness:

Leader: Before we work with God to challenge the injustices of our world, let us confess our own sins. Forgive us, Lord, for all the wrong we have done and for the good we have failed to do. Keep us from false pride in our own righteousness.

Response: Forgive us, Lord.

God has had mercy on us, and because of the suffering, death, and resurrection of Christ, he forgives us all of our sins. That forgiveness is also promised for all who are responsible for the injustices, pain, and conflict in our world.

Scripture Lesson:

Lessons are read from the Prophets, Letters, and the Gospels. They may be selected around the action or event to highlight a given social problem to be addressed. Discussion can then take place on understanding God's role and ours in addressing the concerns.

The Prayers:

Leader: Let us pray for many we know who are suffering injustice, pain, and loneliness.

For the poor who worry about shelter, food, and health concerns.

Response: Bring them the help they need.

Leader: For the sick who seek relief from worry, pain, and weakness.

Response: Heal all those who suffer pain in body and mind.

Leader: For refugees and migrants who seek a new life in a strange land and may face hatred and deportation.

Response: Help us befriend the strangers in our midst.

Leader: For political prisoners and those captive in their jobs and relationships.

Response: Bring them patience, liberation, and freedom.

Leader: For all who suffer discrimination because of race and gender in work and society.

Response: Help us all to value the importance and worth of all people you have made and love.

Leader: All this we ask in the name of Jesus who works, sometimes through us, to bring justice, healing, and equality to all of his people.

The Meal:

Leader: The first Lord's Supper was a preparation for suffering, death, denial, and struggle. It was celebrated with very imperfect individuals who before their flight bragged about who was the greatest. Yet, as they lived out their mission, they changed the world. They often returned to the Lord's Supper for forgiveness, for strength to meet their challenges, and for the fellowship of those who remembered Christ's death and resurrection.

Our Lord Jesus Christ, on the night he was betrayed, took bread, and when he had given thanks, he broke it and gave it to his disciples, saying, "Take, eat, this is my body, which is given for you. This do in remembrance of me."

In the same way, he also took the cup after supper, and when he had given thanks, he gave it to them, saying, "Drink of it, all of you. This is the new covenant in my blood, which is shed for you for the forgiveness of sins; this do as often as you drink it in remembrance of me."

Sharing the Bread and Cup:

They offer each other the bread and wine, saying, "Take, eat, the body of Christ.—Take, drink, the blood of Christ."

Blessing:

Leader: May the body and blood of our Lord Jesus Christ strengthen and preserve us in body and soul unto life everlasting.

Response: Thank you, Lord, for giving us of yourself in this holy meal. Refresh our faith and inspire us to love our neighbors in this time of uncertainty and need. In Jesus' name we pray.

Leader: May our Father bless us and all the vulnerable people around us that need our concern and help. May Jesus continue to show his love toward us and through us. May the Spirit give us new insight into how God is working in our world and new energy to have him work through us.

Response: Amen.

Chapter 8

The Wedding

"This bridal banquet is great but when do we get to meet the groom?" asked the young lady. "He is just waiting until the day of the wedding," said the host. He has been with us in spirit, but we are going to see him face to face. While most of us fear our death and do not even want to think about it, it is really the wedding with our groom. He is the one who has provided us with this banquet. Looking at it from his point of view, our death is beyond gloom; it is the open door to joy.

At the first Lord's Supper, after all had communed, Jesus said, "I will never drink of this fruit of the vine until I drink it new with you in my Father's kingdom" (Matt 26:29). Here Jesus, knowing the death that awaited him, looked beyond it to the wedding banquet, where he would be eating and drinking with us in a far better place. The communion service here and now is just a foretaste of the wedding and the feast to come. While the Lord's Supper provides forgiveness, community, and a taste of the divine in this life, it only anticipates the joy of being joined with Christ in our future. What will that be like?

The Kingdom of God

The first recorded words of Jesus were, "The kingdom of God has come near; repent, and believe in the good news" (Mark 1:15). Then Jesus said that the kingdom was near. At the wedding feast, Jesus will say, "The kingdom of God is here." When communion is at a church about to close its doors, it is a sad event. At a soup kitchen, many of the poor will go back to their tents on that vacant lot. At the refugee camp, there is the terrible wait for enough food and for a bit of hope that somewhere a home and refuge will be found. At every communion service, there is still a sense that this is a bit of salvation from that which is incomplete, very sad, and still bad.

Jesus began to fulfill the promises of the prophets for the coming kingdom. He forgave the sin of the paralytic; he healed the lepers, the sick, and the lame. He made the blind to see and the deaf to hear. He praised the enemy commander and a woman of another people for their faith. He raised from the dead Lazarus and a young girl. He fed the four thousand and the five thousand. These were marvelous works for which people praised him and became his followers. Yet, as worthy as they were, they were not complete. People still died of sickness, hunger, shame, and thirst. The kingdom of God was near, but it was not totally here. This was behind Jesus' words at the Last Supper, "I will never drink of this fruit of the vine until I drink it new with you in my Father's kingdom" (Matt 26:29).

In the Father's kingdom, there will be no more homeless people. Everyone will finally be at home. No one will be hungry or thirsty; no one will be disabled. All the blind will see, and the deaf will hear. All pain will be gone. There will be no more prisons, no unrewarded labor. Those who were poor will have as much as the rich and the rich will have no more than the poor. War will be no more, and death will have been abolished. The blessings of the kingdom on earth gave us a bit of hope. Maybe things might get better than we thought. Now in the Father's kingdom they will have gotten much, much better. In fact, everything is perfect.

The Groom

When Jesus referred to himself as the bridegroom (Matt 9:15), it had been quite a day. He had been surrounded by crowds. Just to get Jesus to help, some actually opened up a roof so that they could lower down a paralyzed man in front of Jesus. Jesus then forgave him his sins and healed him. Jesus' critics were incensed that Jesus would forgive sins. Then Jesus saw Matthew, a tax collector, at his work and called him to be his follower. Amazingly Matthew got up and followed him. Later Matthew threw a large reception for Jesus, inviting some of his despised tax collector friends. Then in the midst of eating and drinking the critics again berated him for not fasting as did some of the disciples of John. But Jesus had the last word. You do not fast when the bridegroom is with you. What would a wedding be like if that was the custom? No, when the bridegroom is missing, then you may fast (Luke 5:16–35).

What will it be like when we meet our bridegroom after our death has been abolished? Yes, maybe our passing was a bit like being paralyzed and let down through the roof. Then he will say again, "Your sins are forgiven," as he heals every one of our ills. For the Matthews among us who have been "public sinners," he says, "Follow me." And we have all come. Now there is the reception, the wedding party, the best food and wine. The bridegroom is with us, and he is ours. He is good-looking, of course. Still, if one looks closely, there are still the little scars on his hand, reminders of the nails that fixed him to the cross. The love he has had for us is still visible. Now he is ours.

As they say, "It is a marriage made in heaven." Unlike many on earth, this one will be perfect. There will be no arguments, no disappointments, and no infidelities. His love is secure, and he showers it upon us. We need never wonder if his love will fade or his attention might be drawn elsewhere. Now even our real beauty and dignity are revealed. John writes, "Let us rejoice and be glad and give the glory to him, for the marriage of the Lamb has come and his bride has made herself ready. And it was given to her to clothe herself in fine linen, bright and clean; for the fine linen is the righteous acts of the saints. And he said to me, 'Write this: "Blessed are those who are invited to the marriage supper of the Lamb"'" (Rev 19:7–9). For those on earth who have looked for the perfect relationship, a place where our heart is at home, it is here.

The Honeymoon

Speaking of the resurrection, Jesus said that people neither marry nor are given in marriage (Matt 22:30). Earthly marriage is no more. Yet, all of us there, the multitudes of times past and present, are together the bride of Christ. The roots of that mystery are found already in the Lord's Supper we celebrate here on earth. St. Paul says that we will be judged if we do not discern the Lord's body (1 Cor 11:29). In the following chapter, Paul says that we are the body of Christ and individually members of it (1 Cor 12:27). At that great wedding in heaven the body of Christ, now purified, now working all together, is the bride of Christ. Paul had been addressing some of the divisions in the church between people with different gifts and roles. Each one was needed in the body of Christ; each had value, respect, and an honored place.

Here the church was to be a model for the world, hopelessly split by language, race, nationality, and economic inequality. If the church, here on earth, could come together as one body, there was at least some hope for the world. Alas, with divisions in congregations, denominations, and among the world fellowship of churches, that is still beyond reach. But at the wedding with the groom, the bride is beautiful, loved by the groom, and clothed in the righteousness of the saints. Given the anger, conflict, hatred, and violence in our world, that picture of a perfect body, working together, each doing their part, is one of the most beautiful pictures of the life to come.

At the very beginning of what was to be a perfect marriage Genesis states, "For this cause a man shall leave his father and his mother and shall cleave to his wife; and they shall become one flesh. And the man and his wife were both naked and were not ashamed" (Gen 2:24–25). In the divine honeymoon, as the very body of Christ, we are one flesh. To be at one with Christ has long been a spiritual goal of mystics and even ordinary folk who have hungered for the peace in the soul which that would bring. Yet here, it has always eluded us as an impossible dream. Yet, as we look ahead, it is there waiting for us. We will be perfectly joined together with Christ, one body, and one flesh.

With that vision of the coming kingdom, our beloved groom, the body of Christ, and the perfect honeymoon, our communion takes on a new meaning. It is a very simple thing, with very earthly bread and wine, and shared with fallible human beings. Yet it has within it the roots of a wedding feast beyond our fondest hopes. This appetizer is truly a foretaste of the feast to come.

Conclusion

A CHANGE IN COMMUNION practices toward a more biblical model can have profound consequences to the church and in the world. By blessing lay people without a professional theological education to administer Holy Communion, churches are free from the necessity to raise money to support the church. Any group of Christians can be the church without funds for the support of clergy at that place. The church is also free from the necessity of paying for the construction and upkeep of a building in a missionary setting. Furthermore, when gathered as a small group with locally administered communion, more contributions can be used for helping the vulnerable.

With approximately 45,000 Christian denominations in the world, moves toward greater Christian unity are very important. In the past some new denominations were formed to bring about this unity. International organizations like the World Council of Churches and the World Evangelical Alliance have sought to be umbrella organizations fostering greater cooperation. At the local level Bible study fellowships have often brought together people from different traditions. However, without communion uniting these people into one church, they usually identify themselves with the church from which they came. Now, however, in a house church, with both the teaching and sharing of the word of God and the celebration of communion, the movement toward greater Christian unity takes gigantic leap forward. Since that local community is already made up of people from different denominations, hopefully they will be the first to recognize the totality of the Christian church on earth.

With Holy Communion at the very center of their efforts, some groups can devote themselves to specific prophetic works of radically addressing some social problems as did the Hebrew prophets or Christ himself. Without depending upon financial contributions to support their ministry, such groups are free to address the inequality of wealth, the sins of nationalism, and specifics of environmental destruction. Other small, sometimes *ad hoc* communities can devote their efforts to special needs in healthcare, education, refugee relief, housing, and other struggles. In the past, centered in the Eucharist, Roman Catholic monasteries and nunneries were able carry out some of these ministries. Now with Holy Communion again as the inspiring and equipping center of their activities, groups made up of lay people from a variety of backgrounds can join to accomplish some significant ministries.

The Lord's Supper was instituted by Christ to create a new covenant with sinners, redeemed and forgiven by Christ. Joined together both by their sin and their salvation, Holy Communion was designed to bring people together to carry out their ministries as part of the very body of Christ. In the past, communion has divided God's people across the centuries. Now, can it be celebrated to unite us?

Appendix

THE IDEA THAT LAY people might celebrate the Lord's Supper without the benefit of clergy owes much to Roland Allen. He was an Anglican priest who came out of the high church tradition of that church body which elevated the importance of the sacrament in worship. However, as a missionary to China from 1895–1903 he came to realize that the biblical example of elders celebrating the Lord's Supper might be a better way of doing mission work than was being done by churches and missionary societies of that time. After his return from China, he spent much of his time writing about his convictions. Below is a partial list of his writings as well as many commentators who have found inspiration in his work and a new direction for the mission work of the church. I have also included some books on contemporary house churches.

This author had the opportunity to visit with Hubert Allen, the grandson of Allen. Together we examined an unpublished manuscript of Allen at the Bodleian Library at Oxford University in the United Kingdom. It was entitled *The Ministry of Expansion: The Priesthood of the Laity*. It has recently been published with commentary and is listed below.

APPENDIX

Works by Roland Allen

"Case for Voluntary Clergy." In *Ministry of the Spirit*, edited by David Paton. Grand Rapids: Eerdmans, 1952.
"Devolution—The Question of the Hour." *World Dominion* 5.3 (July 1927).
"Essentials of an Indigenous Church." *Chinese Recorder* (August 1925).
"Islam and Christianity in the Sudan." *International Review of Missions* (October 1925).
Ministry of Expansion: The Priesthood of the Laity. Edited by J. D. Payne. Pasadena: William Carey, 2017.
"Mission Activities Considered in Relation to the Manifestation of the Spirit." In *Ministry of the Spirit*, edited by David Paton. Grand Rapids: Eerdmans, 1952.
Missionary Methods: St. Paul's or Ours? London: World Dominion, 1956.
"Montessori Method and Missionary Methods." *International Review of Missions* (April 1913).
"Non-Professional Missionaries." In *Ministry of the Spirit*, edited by David Paton. Grand Rapids: Eerdmans, 1952.
"Place of Medical Missions." *World Dominion* 8.1 (January 1930).
S. I. W. Clark, the Man Who Saw the Truth About Foreign Missions. London: World Dominion, 1937.
Spontaneous Expansion of the Church and the Causes Which Hinder It. Grand Rapids: Eerdmans, 1952.

Works About Allen and His Relevance

Allen, Hubert. *Roland Allen: Pioneer, Priest, and Prophet*. Grand Rapids: Eerdmans, 1995.
Boer, Harry. "Roland Allen—Voice in the Wilderness." *World Dominion* (July–August) 1934.
Grubb, Kenneth. Foreword to *The Spontaneous Expansion of the Church and the Causes Which Hinder It*. Grand Rapids: Eerdmans, 1952.
Goodall, Norman, and Eric Nielson. *Survey of the Training of the Ministry in Africa, Part III*. London: International Missionary Council, 1954.
Neill, Stephen. *The Unfinished Task*. London: Edinburgh House, 1957.
Newbigin, Leslie. Foreword to *Roland Allen, Pioneer, Priest, and Prophet*. Grand Rapids: Eerdmans, 1995.
Paton, David. *Missions Under the Judgment of God*. London: SCM, 1953.
Payne, J. D. *Roland Allen, Pioneer of Spontaneous Expansion*. CreateSpace, 2012.
———. "Roland Allen, Missiology and the Ministry of Expansion." In *Ministry of Expansion: The Priesthood of the Laity*, edited by J. D. Payne. Pasadena: William Carey, 2017.

APPENDIX

Rutt, Stephen. "An Analysis of Roland Allen's Missionary Ecclesiology." *Transformation: An International Journal of Holistic Mission Studies* 29.3 (July 2012).

———. "Roland Allen's Apostolic Principles: An Analysis of His 'Ministry of Expansion.'" *Transformation: An International Journal of Holistic Mission Studies* 29.3 (July 2012).

Schmidt, Robert. "Roland Allen and the Coming Kingdom." *Transformation: An International Journal of Holistic Mission Studies* 29.3 (July 2012).

———. "The Ministry of Expansion and Contemporary Crises." In *Ministry of Expansion: The Priesthood of the Laity*, edited by J. D. Payne. Pasadena: William Carey, 2017.

Talltorp, Ake. *Sacrament and Growth: A Study in the Sacramental Dimension of Expansion in the Life of the Local Church, as Reflected in the Theology of Roland Allen*. Uppsala: Swedish Institute for Missionary Research, 1989.

———. "Sacraments for Growth in Mission: Eucharistic Faith and Practice in the Theology of Roland Allen." *Transformation: An International Journal of Holistic Mission Studies* 29.3 (July 2012).

New Forms of the Ministry

Reflecting on Allen's insights or simply seeking to meet the challenges of the situation, below are just a few examples of Christian communities around the world using new forms of ministry in India, among the Maasai, and in the Amazon region.

Bharati, Dayanand. *Living Water and Indian Bowl: An Analysis of Christian Failings in Communicating Christ to Hindus, with Suggestions Toward Improvements*. Pasadena: William Carey, 2004.

Donovan, Vincent. *Christianity Rediscovered*. New York: Orbis, 1978.

Olson, Bruce. *Bruchko*. Lake Mary, FL: Charisma, 1973.

House Churches

Partridge, Dale, ed. *How We Do House Church: The Biblical Doctrines and Convictions of Reformation Fellowship*. Sedona, AZ: Relearn, 2020.

Payne, J. D. *Missional House Churches: Reaching Our Communities with the Gospel*. Downers Grove, IL: InterVarsity, 2007.

Shepperd, Jason. *A Church of House Churches: An Articulated and Applied Ecclesiology*. Woodlands, TX: Good City, 2022.

Simpson, Wolfgang. *Houses that Change the World: The Return of House Churches*. Emmelsbüll: OM, 2011.

Zdero, Rad. *The Global House Church Movement*. Pasadena: William Carey, 2004.

Bibliography

Allen, Roland. *Missionary Methods: St. Paul's or Ours?* London: World Dominion, 1956.

———. "The Case for Voluntary Clergy." In *The Ministry of the Spirit*, edited by David Paton, 61–90. Grand Rapids: Eerdmans, 1962.

Luther, Martin. *Luther's Works* 53. Philadelphia: Fortress, 1965.

World Council of Churches. *Baptism, Eucharist, and Ministry*. Geneva: World Council of Churches, 1982.

www.ingramcontent.com/pod-product-compliance
Lightning Source LLC
LaVergne TN
LVHW021617080426
835510LV00019B/2614